The Little Box of Knitted Throws
© 2005 by Martingale & Company

Martingale & Company
20205 144th Avenue NE
Woodinville, WA 98072-8478
www.martingale-pub.com

Printed in China
10 09 08 07 06 05   8 7 6 5 4 3 2

D0904105

CREDITS

President • Nancy J. Martin
CEO • Daniel J. Martin
VP and General Manager • Tom Wierzbicki
Publisher • Jane Hamada
Editorial Director • Mary V. Green
Managing Editor • Tina Cook
Technical Editor • Ursula Reikes
Copy Editor • Liz McGehee
Design Director • Stan Green
Illustrator • Robin Strobel
Cover and Text Designer • Regina Girard
Photo Stylists: Regina Girard
and Ursula Reikes
Photographer • Brent Kane

MISSION STATEMENT

Dedicated to providing quality products and service to inspire creativity.

We wish to thank the following knitters for their time and talent in making the throws:

Mary Green: Garden Gate, Rhythm in Blue, Pretty in Pink

Virginia Lauth: Arbor, Holiday Sampler

Byrle I. McCart: The Men's Club

Jan Moore: Easy Aran Squares, Cabin Cozy

Ursula Reikes: Confetti, Baby Blocks, Sunset Squares, Stained Glass

JoAn Reynolds: Triple Wave, Butterfly Wings

Jan Runkel: Mocha Ripple, Tri-Color Weave

Karen Costello Soltys: School Spirit, Spring Lace

Robin Strobel: Ruby Knights, Diamonds in Denim

Crocheted Edges

Several of the throws call for 2 or more rounds of crochet around the entire edge. Because crochet stitches are denser than knit stitches, the edges of the throw can become rippled if the crochet stitches are not worked evenly along the edges. When working the first row of crochet, start by working 1 crochet stitch in each stitch or end of row. If the edge appears to be rippling, try crocheting in 2 out of every 3 stitches or rows, or 3 out of every 4 stitches or rows. Consider a different size crochet hook if you have trouble achieving the correct tension.

Work 3 stitches (in same stitch as the round) in each corner stitch. Join the rounds with a slip stitch in the beginning stitch. Fasten off at the end of the last round. Do not turn the work unless the directed to do so. On subsequent rounds, work 1 stitch in each stitch from the previous row, except for the corners, where you will work 3 stitches. Work into both loops of the stitches from the previous round unless otherwise instructed.

Standard Yarn-Weight System

Yarn Weight Symbol and Category Names	**1** SUPER FINE	**2** FINE	**3** LIGHT	**4** MEDIUM	**5** BULKY	**6** SUPER BULKY
Types of Yarns in Category	Sock, Fingering, Baby	Sport, Baby	DK, Light Worsted	Worsted, Afghan, Aran	Chunky, Craft, Rug	Bulky, Roving
Knit Gauge Ranges in Stockinette to 4"	27 to 32 sts	23 to 26 sts	21 to 24 sts	16 to 20 sts	12 to 15 sts	6 to 11 sts
Recommended Needle in Metric Size Range	2.25 to 3.25 mm	3.25 to 3.75 mm	3.75 to 4. 5 mm	4.5 to 5.5 mm	5.5 to 8 mm	8 mm and larger
Recommended Needle in U.S. Size Range	1 to 3	3 to 5	5 to 7	7 to 9	9 to 11	11 and larger

Yarn Conversion

Use these handy formulas for easy conversions.

Yards x 0.9144 = meters
Meters x 1.0936 = yards

Grams x 0.0352 = ounces
Ounces x 28.35 = grams

Joining Squares

Use these instructions to join the squares in Easy Aran Squares on card 17.

To join squares, place 2 squares side by side with right sides facing up and cables at right angles to each other. With slip knot on crochet hook and working yarn underneath and between the 2 squares, *insert hook from right side through both loops at edge on first square, yarn over and pull through stitch (2 loops on hook), insert hook from right side through both loops of corresponding stitch on second square, yarn over and pull through stitch (3 loops on hook), yarn over and pull through all 3 loops, repeating from * to end. Remember to keep the working yarn underneath and between the squares.

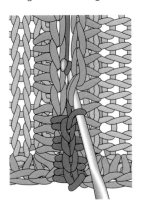 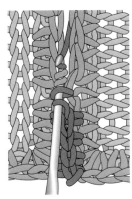

Overcast Stitch

Place squares next to each other with right sides facing up. With crochet hook and strand of yarn, insert hook from back to front in back loop of first edge stitch at corner of first square, leaving a 3" tail, then insert hook from back to front into back loop of corresponding corner stitch on second square. *Insert hook from front to back into back loop of next stitch on first square, then insert hook from back to front of next stitch on second square; draw yarn through but don't pull too tight.* A short diagonal line will appear between the back loops of the 2 squares. Repeat from * to * to end of squares; fasten off and weave in ends.

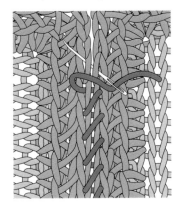

Contents

Abbreviations and Glossary

approx	approximately
beg	begin(ning)
BO	bind off
ch	chain
cn	cable needle
CO	cast on
cont	continue
dc	double crochet
dec	decrease
g	grams
hdc	half double crochet
inc	increase
K	knit
K1f&b	knit 1 stitch through front loop and 1 stitch through back loop of same stitch
K2tog	knit 2 stitches together
M1	make 1 stitch: make new stitch by lifting horizontal bar between 2 stitches from front to back with left needle and knitting into back of loop
P	purl
p2sso	pass 2 slipped stitches over
P2tog	purl 2 stitches together
patt	pattern
pm	place marker
PU	pick up and knit
RS	right side
rem	remain(ing)
rep	repeat(ing)
rnd(s)	round(s)
sc	single crochet
sl	slip
ssk	slip, slip, knit: slip 2 stitches 1 at a time as if to knit, knit these 2 stitches together
st(s)	stitch(es)
St st	stockinette stitch: knit on RS rows, purl on WS rows
tog	together
WS	wrong side
wyib	with yarn in back
wyif	with yarn in front
yds	yards
YO	yarn over

Garden Gate

Gorgeous texture and soft, chunky wool make this the perfect throw to snuggle under on the coldest winter days.

APPROXIMATE SIZE
39" x 56"

MATERIALS
7 skeins of Magnum from Cascade Yarns (100% wool; 123 yds; 250 g), color 9338

Size 13 circular needle (29" or longer) or size required to obtain gauge

GAUGE
8 sts = 4" in patt

GATEPOST PATTERN
(Multiple of 12 + 6)

Row 1 (RS): K2, P1, *P1, K2, P6, K2, P1, rep from * to last 3 sts, P1, K2.

Row 2 and all WS rows: Knit the knit sts and purl the purl sts.

Row 3: K2, P1, *P1, K10, P1, rep from * to last 3 sts, P1, K2.

Row 5: K3, *K5, P2, K5, rep from * to last 3 sts, K3.

Row 7: P3, *P3, K2, P2, K2, P3, rep from * to last 3 sts, P3.

Row 9: Rep row 5.

Row 11: Rep row 3.

Row 12: Knit the knit sts and purl the purl sts.

Rep rows 1–12.

DIRECTIONS
- CO 78 sts. Work in Gatepost patt until piece measures approx 56", ending with completed row 12.
- BO sts loosely.
- Block.

Rhythm in Blue

The undulating flame pattern of this throw really shines when stitched in a single bold color.

APPROXIMATE SIZE
48" x 60"

MATERIALS
12 skeins of Pastaza from Cascade Yarns (50% llama, 50% wool; 132 yds; 100 g), color 1019 Royal Blue

Size 10 circular needle (29") or size required to obtain gauge

GAUGE
15 sts = 4" in patt

SEED STITCH
Row 1 (RS): *K1, P1, rep from *.

Row 2: Knit the purl sts and purl the knit sts.

Rep row 2.

FLAME WAVE PATTERN
(Multiple of 7 + 5)

Row 1 and all WS rows: Purl.

Row 2 (RS): K4, *ssk, K5, M1, rep from * to last st, K1.

Row 4: K4, *ssk, K4, M1, K1, rep from * to last st, K1.

Row 6: K4, *ssk, K3, M1, K2, rep from * to last st, K1.

Row 8: K4, *ssk, K2, M1, K3, rep from * to last st, K1.

Row 10: K4, *ssk, K1, M1, K4, rep from * to last st, K1.

Row 12: K4, *ssk, M1, K5, rep from * to last st, K1.

Row 14: K1, *M1, K5, K2tog, rep from * to last 4 sts, K4.

Row 16: K1, *K1, M1, K4, K2tog, rep from * to last 4 sts, K4.

Row 18: K1, *K2, M1, K3, K2tog, rep from * to last 4 sts, K4.

Row 20: K1, *K3, M1, K2, K2tog, rep from * to last 4 sts, K4.

Row 22: K1, *K4, M1, K1, K2tog, rep from * to last 4 sts, K4.

Row 24: K1, *K5, M1, K2tog, rep from * to last 4 sts, K4.

DIRECTIONS
- CO 180 sts and work in seed st for 11 rows.
- On next RS row, beg Flame Wave patt and work in patt until throw measures approx 58", ending with completed row 12 or 24.
- Work 11 rows in seed st.
- BO sts loosely.
- Block gently.

Spring Lace

Light as a feather and soft as a spring breeze, this fabulous throw practically guarantees sweet dreams.

APPROXIMATE SIZE
48" x 60

MATERIALS
12 skeins of Baby Alpaca Brush from Plymouth Yarn Company (80% alpaca, 20% acrylic; 110 yds, 50 g), color 1477 Celery Green

Size 9 circular needle (40") or size required to obtain gauge

GAUGE
13 sts = 4" in patt

LACY ZIGZAG PATTERN
(Multiple of 6 + 1)

Rows 1, 3, 5 (RS): *Ssk, K2, YO, K2, rep from * to last st, K1.

Row 2 and all WS rows: Purl.

Rows 7, 9, 11: K3, *YO, K2, K2tog, K2, rep from * to last 4 sts, YO, K2, K2tog.

Row 12: Purl.

Rep rows 1–12.

DIRECTIONS
- CO 157 sts and work bottom border as follows:

    Knit 1 row (WS).

    Purl 1 row.

    Knit 2 rows.

    Purl 1 row.

- Beg Lacy Zigzag patt on next RS row and work until piece measures approx 59", ending with completed row 12.

- Work top border as follows:

    Knit 2 rows.

    Purl 1 row.

    Knit 1 row.

- BO sts loosely.

- Block gently.

Arbor

*The twining pattern and openwork on this beautiful
throw are reminiscent of a romantic garden arbor.*

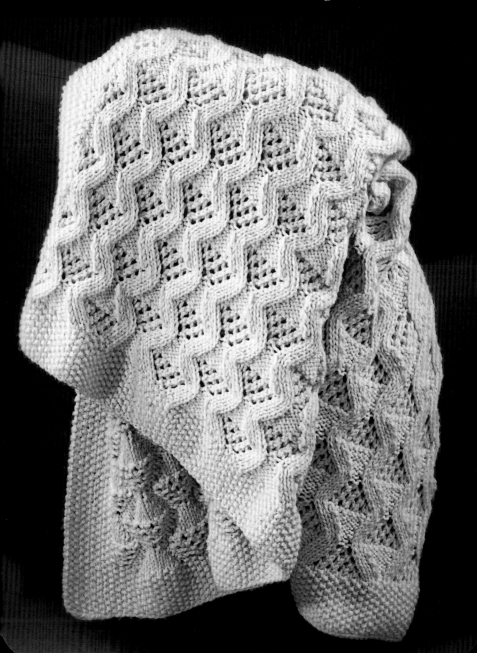

APPROXIMATE SIZE
48" x 60"

MATERIALS
10 skeins of Wool-Ease Chunky from Lion Brand Yarn (80% acrylic, 20% wool; 153 yds; 140 g), color 099 Fisherman

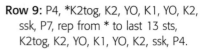
5 BULKY

Size 10 circular needle (32") or size required to obtain gauge

2 ring markers

GAUGE
13 sts = 4" in patt

SEED STITCH
Row 1 (RS): K1, *P1, K1, rep from *.

Row 2: Knit the purl sts and purl the knit sts.

Rep row 2.

ARBOR PATTERN
(Multiple of 16 + 1)

Row 1 (RS): K1, *YO, K2, ssk, P7, K2tog, K2, YO, K1, rep from *.

Row 2: P5, *K7, P9, rep from * to last 12 sts, K7, P5.

Row 3: K2, *YO, K2, ssk, P5, K2tog, K2, YO, K2tog, YO, K1, rep from * to last 15 sts, YO, K2, ssk, P5, K2tog, K2, YO, K2.

Row 4: P6, *K5, P11, rep from * to last 11 sts, K5, P6.

Row 5: *K2tog, YO, K1, YO, K2, ssk, P3, K2tog, K2, YO, K2tog, YO, rep from * to last st, K1.

Row 6: P7, *K3, P13, rep from * to last 10 sts, K3, P7.

Row 7: K1, *K2tog, YO, K1, YO, K2, ssk, P1, K2tog, K2, YO, (K2tog, YO) twice, rep from * to last 16 sts, K2tog, YO, K1, YO, K2, ssk, P1, K2tog, K2, YO, K2tog, YO, K2.

Row 8: P8, *K1, P15, rep from * to last 9 sts, K1, P8.

Row 9: P4, *K2tog, K2, YO, K1, YO, K2, ssk, P7, rep from * to last 13 sts, K2tog, K2, YO, K1, YO, K2, ssk, P4.

Row 10: K4, *P9, K7, rep from * to last 13 sts, P9, K4.

Row 11: P3, *K2tog, K2, YO, K2tog, YO, K1, YO, K2, ssk, P5, rep from * to last 14 sts, K2tog, K2, YO, K2tog, YO, K1, YO, K2, ssk, P3.

Row 12: K3, *P11, K5, rep from * to last 14 sts, P11, K3.

Row 13: P2, *K2tog, K2, YO, (K2tog, YO) twice, K1, YO, K2, ssk, P3, rep from * to last 15 sts, K2tog, K2, YO, (K2tog, YO) twice, K1, YO, K2, ssk, P2.

Row 14: K2, *P13, K3, rep from * to last 15 sts, P13, K2.

Row 15: P1, *K2tog, K2, YO, (K2tog, YO) 3 times, K1, YO, K2, ssk, P1, rep from *.

Row 16: K1, *P15, K1, rep from *.

Rep rows 1–16.

DIRECTIONS
- CO 149 sts and work 3" in seed st.
- Set up patt on next RS row as follows: work 10 sts in seed st, pm, work next 129 sts in Arbor patt, pm, work 10 sts in seed st. Cont in established patt, keeping first 10 sts and last 10 sts in seed st until piece measures approx 57", ending with completed row 16 of Arbor patt.
- Work 3" in seed st. BO all sts.
- Block.

Pretty in Pink

. . . or in any other color! This easy pattern stitches up quickly for a great room accent.

APPROXIMATE SIZE
48" x 56"

MATERIALS
11 skeins of 128 from Cascade
  Yarns (100% wool; 220 yds;
  100 g), color 380 Pink

Size 10 circular needle (29") or size
  required to obtain gauge

2 ring markers

GAUGE
13 sts = 4" in patt

GARTER STITCH
Knit every row.

WIDE DIAGONAL-RIB PATTERN
(Multiple of 8)

Row 1 (RS): *P6, K2, rep from *.

Row 2 and all WS rows: Knit the knit sts
and purl the purl sts.

Row 3: P5, K2, *P6, K2, rep from * to
last st, P1.

Row 5: P4, K2, *P6, K2, rep from * to
last 2 sts, P2.

Row 7: P3, K2, *P6, K2, rep from * to
last 3 sts, P3.

Row 9: P2, K2, *P6, K2, rep from * to
last 4 sts, P4.

Row 11: P1, K2, *P6, K2, rep from * to
last 5 sts, P5.

Row 13: K2, *P6, K2, rep from * to last 6
sts, P6.

Row 15: K1, *P6, K2, rep from * to last 7
sts, P6, K1.

Row 16: Rep row 2.

Rep rows 1–16.

DIRECTIONS
- CO 158 sts and work 2 rows in garter
  st, then work in St st until piece measures 2", ending with completed WS
  row.

- Set up patt st on next RS row as
  follows: K7, pm, work next 144 sts in
  Wide Diagonal-Rib patt, pm, K7. Cont in
  established patt, keeping first 7 sts and
  last 7 sts in St st until piece measures
  approx 54", ending with row 16.

- Work in St st for 1¾", then work 2
  rows of garter st. BO sts loosely.

- Block.

Butterfly Wings

Soft and sweet, this throw is perfect
for a nursery or little girl's room.

APPROXIMATE SIZE
42" x 48"

MATERIALS
9 skeins of Encore Chunky from Plymouth Yarn Company (75% acrylic, 25% wool; 143 yds; 100 g), color 215 Yellow

Size 10 circular needle (29") or size required to obtain gauge

Size G crochet hook

GAUGE
16 sts = 4" in patt

BUTTERFLY WINGS PATTERN
(Multiple of 26)

Row 1 and every WS row: Purl.

Row 2 (RS): K1, *M1, ssk, K4, K2tog, K3, M1, K2, M1, K3, ssk, K4, K2tog, M1, K2, rep from *, ending last rep with K1 instead of K2.

Row 4: K1, *M1, K1, ssk, K2, K2tog, K4, M1, K2, M1, K4, ssk, K2, K2tog, K1, M1, K2, rep from *, ending last rep with K1 instead of K2.

Row 6: K1, *M1, K2, ssk, K2tog, K5, M1, K2, M1, K5, ssk, K2tog, K2, M1, K2, rep from *, ending last rep with K1 instead of K2.

Row 8: K1, *M1, K3, ssk, K4, K2tog, M1, K2, M1, ssk, K4, K2tog, K3, M1, K2, rep from *, ending last rep with K1 instead of K2.

Row 10: K1, *M1, K4, ssk, K2, K2tog, K1, M1, K2, M1, K1, ssk, K2, K2tog, K4, M1, K2, rep from *, ending last rep with K1 instead of K2.

Row 12: K1, *M1, K5, ssk, K2tog, (K2, M1) twice, K2, ssk, K2tog, K5, M1, K2, rep from *, ending last rep with K1 instead of K2.

Rep rows 1–12.

DIRECTIONS
- CO 156 sts and work in Butterfly Wings patt until piece measures approx 45", ending with completed row 12. BO sts loosely.

- **Edging:** With crochet hook and RS facing you, work 1 rnd of sc, turn work. Work 1 rnd of sc (see card 22).

- Block.

Diamonds in Denim

*Bulky yarn worked in an easy knit-and-purl
pattern creates a lapful of texture.*

APPROXIMATE SIZE
44" x 54"

MATERIALS
15 skeins of Blizzard from Reynolds (65% alpaca, 35% acrylic; 66 yds; 100 g), color 683 Indigo

Size 15 circular needle (32") or size required to obtain gauge

2 ring markers

GAUGE
9 sts = 4" in patt

SEED STITCH
Row 1 (RS): K1, *P1, K1, rep from *.

Row 2: Knit the purl sts and purl the knit sts.

Rep row 2.

KNIT AND PURL DIAMOND PATTERN
(Multiple of 10 + 1)

Row 1 (RS): *K5, P1, K4, rep from * to last st, K1.

Row 2 and all WS rows: Knit the knit sts and purl the purl sts.

Row 3: *K4, P3, K3, rep from * to last st, K1.

Row 5: *K3, P5, K2, rep from * to last st, K1.

Row 7: *K2, P7, K1, rep from * to last st, K1.

Row 9: *K1, P9, rep from * to last st, K1.

Row 11: Rep row 7.

Row 13: Rep row 5.

Row 15: Rep row 3.

Row 16: Rep row 2.

Rep rows 1–16.

DIRECTIONS
- CO 99 sts and work 6 rows in seed st.
- Set up patt on next RS row as follows: Work first 4 sts in seed st, pm, work next 91 sts in Knit and Purl Diamond patt, pm, work last 4 sts in seed st. Cont in established patt, working first 4 and last 4 sts in seed st until throw measures approx 51½", ending with completed row 16 of Knit and Purl Diamond patt. Work rows 1 and 2 of Knit and Purl Diamond patt once more.
- Work 6 rows in seed st.
- BO sts loosely.
- Block.

Card 15 • Diamonds in Denim
www.martingale-pub.com • 1-800-426-3126

Ruby Knights

*Alternating knit and purl squares work up
quickly into a rich chessboard pattern.*

APPROXIMATE SIZE
50" x 56"

MATERIALS
10 skeins of Wool-Ease Thick & Quick from Lion Brand Yarn (86% acrylic, 10% wool, 4% rayon; 108 yds; 170 g), color 138 Cranberry

6 SUPER BULKY

Size 15 circular needle (32") or size required to obtain gauge

Size L crochet hook

GAUGE
9 sts = 4" in patt

CHESSBOARD PATTERN
(Multiple of 12 + 1)

Rows 1, 3, 5: *K7, P5, rep from * to last st, K1.

Row 2 and all even-numbered rows: Knit the knit sts and purl the purl sts.

Rows 7, 9, 11: K1, *P5, K7, rep from *.

Row 12: Rep row 2.

Rep rows 1–12.

DIRECTIONS
- CO 109 sts. Beg Chessboard patt and work rows 1–12 a total of 16 times.
- BO sts loosely.
- **Edging:** With crochet hook and RS facing you, work 2 rnds of sc (see card 22).
- Block.

Baby Blocks

Quick-to-stitch blocks are made one at a time and then sewn together in this pretty baby throw.

APPROXIMATE SIZE
35" x 43"

MATERIALS
Encore from Plymouth Yarn Company (75% wool, 25% acrylic; 200 yds; 100 g) in the following amounts and colors:

Blue	2 skeins	color 793
Yellow	2 skeins	color 896
Pink	2 skeins	color 029
Aqua	2 skeins	color 1201

Size 8 needles or size required to obtain gauge

Size G crochet hook

Tapestry needle

GAUGE
17 sts = 4" in seed st and garter st

SEED STITCH
Row 1: *K1, P1, rep from *.

Row 2: Knit the purl sts and purl the knit sts.

Rep row 2.

GARTER STITCH
Knit every row.

DIRECTIONS
- Make 1 square (7½" x 7½") as follows:

  With Blue, CO 32 sts, and work 18 rows in seed st.

  Switch to Yellow and work 20 rows in garter st.

  Switch to Blue and knit 1 row, work 17 rows in seed st. BO in patt on next row.

With Aqua and crochet hook, work 1 row sc all around square, working 3 sc in each corner. Work 1 more row of sc all around square, working into back loops only and working 3 sc in each corner. Fasten off and weave in ends.

- Working the garter-st section in Yellow on all squares, make 10 squares each in the following color combinations for a total of 20 squares:
  - Blue seed st, Yellow garter st, Blue seed st
  - Pink seed st, Yellow garter st, Pink seed st

FINISHING
- Arrange squares in 4 rows of 5 squares each. With Aqua and tapestry needle, sew squares tog using an overcast st (see card 21). Join rows in same manner.
- **Edging:** With crochet hook, RS facing you, and Aqua, work 1 rnd of dc in back loop only. Work 1 rnd of sc in back loop only (see card 22).
- Block.

Sunset Squares

*This gorgeous mitered-squares throw glows
with the colors of the evening sky.*

APPROXIMATE SIZE
42" x 50"

MATERIALS
16 skeins of Kureyon from Noro (100% wool; 110 yds; 50 g), color 102

Size 8 needles or size required to obtain gauge

Tapestry needle

Size G crochet hook

GAUGE
16 sts = 4" in patt after blocking

MITERED SQUARE (8" x 8")
Note: Slip first stitch of each right side row with the yarn in back. Slip last stitch of each right side row with the yarn in front, except for the right side rows just before a purl row, where you will slip the last stitch with the yarn in back. The first and last slipped stitches create a nice edge for joining squares through the back loops.

S2kpo: Sl 2 sts tog knitwise, K1, pass the 2 slipped sts over the knit st.

CO 61 sts.

Row 1 (RS): Sl 1 wyib, K28, s2kpo, K28, sl 1 wyif.

Rows 2, 6, 8, 12, 14, 18, 20, 24, 26, 30, 32, 36, 38, 42, 44, 48, 50, 52, 54, 56: Knit.

Row 3: Sl 1 wyib, K27, s2kpo, K27, sl 1 wyib.

Rows 4, 10, 16, 22, 28, 34, 40, 46: Purl.

Row 5: Sl 1 wyib, K26, s2kpo, K26, sl 1 wyif.

Row 7: Sl 1 wyib, K25, s2kpo, K25, sl 1 wyif.

Row 9: Sl 1 wyib, K24, s2kpo, K24, sl 1 wyib.

Row 11: Sl 1 wyib, K23, s2kpo, K23, sl 1 wyif.

Cont RS rows in this manner, working 1 less st before and after the s2kpo until 3 sts rem (row 57).

Row 58: Knit.

Row 59: S2kpo. Fasten off.

DIRECTIONS
- Make 30 squares; you will get 2 squares from each skein.
- Arrange squares in 5 rows of 6 squares each. Sew squares tog in rows using a tapestry needle and an overcast st (see card 21). Join rows in the same manner.
- **Edging:** With crochet hook and RS facing you, work 1 rnd of sc. Work 1 rnd of sc in back loop only (see card 22).
- Block.

The Men's Club

In rich shades of charcoal and cranberry, this hounds-tooth throw will look great draped over his favorite chair.

APPROXIMATE SIZE
48" x 60"

MATERIALS
Wool-Ease Thick & Quick from
  Lion Brand Yarn (80% acrylic,
  20% wool; 108 yds; 170 g)
  in the following amounts
  and colors:

6
SUPER BULKY

  Cranberry 6 skeins color 138
  Charcoal   6 skeins color 49
Size 13 circular needle (29") or size
  required to obtain gauge
2 ring markers

GAUGE
9 sts = 4" in patt

GARTER STITCH
Knit every row.

HOUNDSTOOTH PATTERN
(Multiple of 3)

Row 1 (RS): With Cranberry, K1, *sl 1
  wyib, K2, rep from * to last 2 sts, sl 1
  wyib, K1.

Row 2: Purl.

Row 3: With Charcoal, *sl 1 wyib, K2, rep
  from * to end.

Row 4: Purl.

Rep rows 1–4.

DIRECTIONS
- With Charcoal, CO 108 sts and work
  bottom border in garter st as follows:
  2 rows of Charcoal
  2 rows of Cranberry
  2 rows of Charcoal
  2 rows of Cranberry
  2 rows of Charcoal

Note: Carry yarns along edge, placing
old yarn on top of new yarn and toward
the left.

- Set up patt on next RS row as follows:
  Work first 6 sts in garter st, pm, work
  next 96 sts in Houndstooth patt, pm,
  work last 6 sts in garter st. Work in
  established patt until piece is approx
  57½" from beg, ending with completed row 2.
- Work top border as for bottom border.
  BO sts loosely in Charcoal.
- Block.

Confetti

Bright, cheerful colors and soft, fuzzy textures combine to make a cuddly throw for Baby.

APPROXIMATE SIZE
36" x 44"

MATERIALS
4 skeins of Encore from Plymouth Yarn Company (75% acrylic, 25% wool; 200 yds; 100 g), color 208 White

Eskimo from Stylecraft (100% polyester; 98 yds; 50 g) in the following amounts and colors:

Purple	1 skein	color 5244
Blue	1 skein	color 5480
Jade	1 skein	color 5483
Yellow	1 skein	color 5061
Pink	1 skein	color 5482

Size 9 circular needle (29") or size required to obtain gauge

GAUGE
16 sts = 4" in garter st with Encore

GARTER STITCH
Knit every row.

DIRECTIONS
- With Purple Eskimo, CO 130 sts and work 7 rows in garter st.
- Change to Encore and work rem throw in garter st, alternating yarns as follows:

  28 rows of Encore

  8 rows of Blue Eskimo

  28 rows of Encore

  8 rows of Jade Eskimo

  28 rows of Encore

  8 rows of Yellow Eskimo

  28 rows of Encore

  8 rows of Pink Eskimo

  28 rows of Encore

  8 rows of Purple Eskimo

  28 rows of Encore

  8 rows of Blue Eskimo

  28 rows of Encore

  8 rows of Jade Eskimo

  28 rows of Encore

  8 rows of Yellow Eskimo

  28 rows of Encore

  7 rows of Pink Eskimo

- BO sts loosely.
- Weave in all ends.
- **Edging:** With RS facing you and Blue Eskimo, PU 1 st in each garter ridge along one side. Knit 6 rows. BO sts loosely. With RS facing you and Jade Eskimo, PU 1 st in each garter ridge along opposite side. Knit 6 rows. BO sts loosely.
- Block if necessary.

. . . .

TIP: To keep track of the rows of garter stitch, count the ridges on the right side. One garter ridge equals 2 rows of garter stitch. You should have 14 ridges after working 28 rows of garter stitch. However, because you won't be able to see the garter ridges in the Eskimo yarn, you'll have to rely on a counter to keep track of the rows in Eskimo.

. . . .

Triple Wave

The classic chevron pattern makes a comeback in updated colors and chunky yarn.

APPROXIMATE SIZE
54" x 64"

MATERIALS
Wool-Ease Thick & Quick from
Lion Brand Yarn (86% acrylic,
10% wool, 4% rayon; 108
yds; 170 g) in the following
amounts and colors:

Charcoal 4 skeins color 149

Wheat 4 skeins color 402

Green 4 skeins color 130

Size 13 circular needle (32") or size
required to obtain gauge

GAUGE
11 sts = 4" in patt

CHEVRON PATTERN
(Multiple of 12 + 3)

Row 1 (RS): K1, ssk, *K4, YO, K1, YO,
K4, sl 2 sts tog as if to knit, K1, p2sso;
rep from * to last 12 sts, K4, YO, K1,
YO, K4, K2tog, K1.

Row 2: Purl.

Rep rows 1 and 2.

COLOR SEQUENCE
12 rows of Charcoal

12 rows of Green

12 rows of Wheat

DIRECTIONS
* With Charcoal, CO 147 sts and beg
  Chevron patt. Cont in patt and work
  36-row color sequence a total of 4
  times.
* BO sts loosely.
* Block.

APPROXIMATE SIZE
50" x 60"

MATERIALS
128 Tweed from Cascade Yarns
(100% wool; 128 yds;
100 g) in the following
amounts and colors:

> 5
> BULKY

Purple   7 skeins color 621

Gray   7 skeins color 616

Size 9 circular needle (48") or size
required to obtain gauge

Size G crochet hook

GAUGE
16 sts = 4" in patt

DIAGONAL SLIP-STITCH PATTERN
(Multiple of 3 + 2)

Row 1 (RS): With Purple, K3, sl 1 wyib,
*K2, sl 1 wyib, rep from * to last st, K1.

Row 2 and all WS rows: Purl across, slipping sts of previous row wyif.

Row 3: With Gray, K1, *sl 1 wyib, K2, rep
from * to last st, K1.

Row 5: With Purple, K2, *sl 1 wyib, K2,
rep from * to end.

Row 7: With Gray, K3, sl 1 wyib, *K2, sl 1
wyib, rep from * to last st, K1.

Row 9: With Purple, K1, *sl 1 wyib, K2,
rep from * to last st, K1.

Row 11: With Gray, K2, *sl 1 wyib, K2,
rep from * to end.

Row 12: Purl across, slipping sts of previous row wyif.

Rep rows 1–12.

DIRECTIONS
- With Purple, CO 194 sts and purl 1
  row (WS).
- Beg Diagonal Slip-St patt and work in
  patt until throw measures approx 58",
  ending with Gray purl row. Knit 1 row
  in Purple, then BO .
- **Edging:** With crochet hook and RS
  facing you, work 3 rnds of sc in the
  following color sequence: 1 rnd of
  Purple, 1 rnd of Gray, 1 rnd of Purple
  (see card 22).
- Block.

Mocha Ripple

*Soft, cozy yarns in warm neutral tones
are welcome in any decor.*

APPROXIMATE SIZE
48" x 60"

MATERIALS
Pastaza from Cascade Yarns
(50% llama, 50% wool; 132
yds; 100 g) in the following
amounts and colors:

Medium Brown	6 skeins	color 080
Light Brown	6 skeins	color 004

Size 13 circular needle (32") or size
required to obtain gauge

GAUGE
12 sts = 4" in patt

GARTER-STITCH CHEVRON PATTERN
(Multiple of 11)

Rows 1–5: With Medium Brown, knit.

Row 6 (RS): Change to Light Brown,
*K2tog, K2, K1f&b twice, K3, ssk, rep
from *.

Row 7: Purl.

Rows 8–11: Rep rows 6 and 7 twice.

Row 12: Change to Medium Brown, rep
row 6.

Rep rows 1–12.

DIRECTIONS
- With Medium Brown, CO 143 sts
  loosely.
- Beg Garter-Stitch Chevron patt and
  work until piece measures approx 60",
  ending with completed row 5. Cut the
  yarn when you change from one color
  to the other and weave in ends later.
- BO sts loosely.
- Block.

Tri-Color Weave

This interesting pattern is reminiscent of a woven blanket, but much easier to create!

APPROXIMATE SIZE
46" x 62"

MATERIALS
Encore Chunky from Plymouth Yarn
   Company (75% acrylic, 25%
   wool; 143 yds; 100 g) in the
   following amounts and colors: **5 BULKY**

Navy	4 skeins	color 848
Off-White	8 skeins	color 146
Red	4 skeins	color 9601

Size 11 circular needle (32") or size
   required to obtain gauge

GAUGE
13½ sts = 4" in patt

GARTER STITCH
Knit every row.

RIBBED TWEED STITCH
(Multiple of 6 + 13)

Row 1: K6, *sl 1 wyib, K5, rep from * to
   last 7 sts, sl 1 wyib, K6.

Row 2: Knit across, sl the sl sts of previous row wyif.

Row 3: K9, *sl 1 wyib, K5, rep from * to
   last 10 sts, sl 1 wyib, K9.

Row 4: Knit across, sl the sl sts of previous row wyif.

Rep rows 1–4 a total of 5 times (for a
total of 20 rows) for each color
sequence.

DIRECTIONS
- With Navy, CO 157 sts and work
  garter-st border with 2 rows of each
  color in the following sequence:

     Navy
     Off-White
     Red
     Off-White
     Navy
     Off-White

- Change to Red and work ribbed tweed
  st as follows:

  Rows 1 and 2 in Red

  Rows 3 and 4 in Off-White

  Rep rows 1–4 of ribbed tweed st in this
  color sequence for a total of 20 rows.

- Work ribbed tweed st in 20-row color
  sequence as follows:

  Rows 1 and 2 in Navy

  Rows 3 and 4 in Off-White

- Rep alternating Red and Blue 20-row
  color sequences until you've worked a
  total of 9 Red/Off-White and 9 Blue/
  Off-White sequences, ending with a
  Blue/Off-White sequence. Work 1
  more color sequence in Red/Off-White,
  ending with completed row 18 in Red.

- Work garter-st border with 2 rows of
  each color in the following sequence:

     Off-White
     Navy
     Off-White
     Red
     Off-White
     Navy

- BO sts loosely.

- Block.

Holiday Sampler

*Show off your stitching skills
with this texture-filled sampler.*

Double-Ridged Rib   **Double Moss**   **Diamond Brocade**   **Basket Rib**

APPROXIMATE SIZE
48" x 58"

MATERIALS
Encore Chunky from Plymouth Yarn
  Company (75% acrylic, 25%
  wool; 143 yds; 100 g) in the
  following amounts and colors:

5 BULKY

MC	Off-White	8 skeins	color 146
CC1	Green	4 skeins	color 204
CC2	Red	2 skeins	color 9601

Size 10 circular needle (32") or size
  required to obtain gauge

GAUGE
14 sts = 4" in St st

SEED STITCH
Row 1 (RS): K1, *P1, K1, rep from *.
Row 2: Knit the purl sts and purl the
  knit sts.
Rep row 2.

DOUBLE-RIDGED RIB PATTERN
Rows 1 (RS), 2, 5, 6: Knit.
Rows 3, 8: P1, *K1, P1, rep from *.
Rows 4, 7: K1, *P1, K1, rep from *.
Rep rows 1–8.

DOUBLE MOSS PATTERN
Rows 1(RS), 4: K1, *P1, K1, rep from *.
Rows 2, 3: P1, *K1, P1, rep from *.
Rep rows 1–4.

DIAMOND BROCADE PATTERN
Row 1 (RS): K4, *P1, K7, rep from * to
  last 5 sts, P1, K4.
Rows 2, 8: P3, *K1, P1, K1, P5, rep from
  * to last 6 sts, K1, P1, K1, P3.
Rows 3, 7: K2, *P1, K3, rep from * to last
  3 sts, P1, K2.
Rows 4, 6: P1, *K1, P5, K1, P1, rep from *.

Row 5: *P1, K7, rep from * to last st, P1.
Rep rows 1–8.

BASKET RIB PATTERN
Row 1 (RS): Knit.
Row 2: Purl.
Row 3: K1, *sl 1 wyib, K1, rep from *.
Row 4: K1, *sl 1 wyif, K1, rep from *.
Rep rows 1–4.

STRIPE A
6 rows CC1, 4 rows CC2, 6 rows CC1

STRIPE B
6 rows CC2, 4 rows CC1, 6 rows CC2

DIRECTIONS
- With CC1, CO 153 sts and work stripe A
  once in seed st.
- With MC, work Double-Ridged Rib patt
  for 10", end with WS row. Knit 2 rows.
- Work stripe B once in St st.
- With MC, knit 2 rows. Work Double
  Moss patt for 10", end with WS row.
  Knit 2 rows.
- Work stripe A once in St st.
- With MC, knit 2 rows. Work Diamond
  Brocade patt for 10", end with WS row.
  Knit 2 rows.
- Work stripe B once in St st.
- With MC, knit 2 rows. Work Basket Rib
  patt for 10", end with WS row. Knit 2
  rows.
- Work stripe A once as follows: knit first
  row, beg seed st on next row, and work
  in seed st for remainder of stripe. BO
  all sts.
- **Edging:** With CC1, PU sts in every
  other row along one side (approx 165
  sts) and work stripe A once in seed st.
  BO sts loosely. Rep edging on opposite
  side.
- Block.

Easy Aran Squares

Classic cables are stitched a block at a time, making this an ideal take-along project.

APPROXIMATE SIZE
50" x 68"

MATERIALS
18 skeins of Encore Chunky from
  Plymouth Yarn (75% acrylic,
  25% wool; 143 yds; 100 g),
  color 240 Tan Heather

Size 11 circular needles (24") or size
  required to obtain gauge
Cable needle
Size K crochet hook

GAUGE
11 sts = 4" in patt

SQUARE
C4B: Sl 2 sts to cn and hold at back of
  work, K2, K2 from cn.
C8B: Sl 4 sts to cn and hold at back of
  work, K4, K4 from cn.

Note: Rows 4 and 8 are *not* the same;
there is no twist in the large cable on
row 8.

- CO 44 sts and work patt as follows:
    Row 1 (WS): (K3, P2, K3, P4) 3
    times, K3, P2, K3.
    Row 2 (RS) (Inc row): *P3, M1, K2,
    M1, P3, (M1, K1) twice, (K1, M1)
    twice, rep from * 2 more times, P3,
    M1, K2, M1, P3—64 sts.
    Row 3 and all other WS rows: (K3,
    P4, K3, P8) 3 times, K3, P4, K3.
    Row 4: (P3, C4B, P3, C8B) 3 times,
    P3, C4B, P3.
    Row 6: (P3, K4, P3, K8) 3 times, P3,
    K4, P3.
    Row 8: (P3, C4B, P3, K8) 3 times, P3,
    C4B, P3).
    Row 10: Rep row 6.

Rep rows 3–10 until 70 total rows have
been completed, ending with row 6.

Row 71 (Dec row): *K3, (P2tog) twice,
K3, (P2tog) 4 times, rep from * 2 more
times, K3, (P2tog) twice, K3—44 sts.

Next row: BO in patt; do not fasten off.
Place last st from BO on crochet hook,
ch 1, work 1 rnd sc all around square,
working 41 sc on each side and 3 sc
in each corner. Fasten off.

DIRECTIONS
- Make 12 squares.
- Alternating directions of cables, join
  squares into 3 rows of 4 squares each.
  Refer to "Joining Squares" on card 21
  for detailed instructions. Join rows in
  same manner.
- **Edging:** With crochet hook and RS facing you, work 1 rnd of hdc, do not turn
  work. Ch 1, work 1 rnd of sc, working
  in third loop behind and below back
  loop of previous row, turn work. With
  WS facing you, ch 2, work 1 rnd of
  hdc. See card 22.
- Block.

Cabin Cozy

Bring a rustic touch to any room with this inviting throw. The slip-stitch rows add a unique accent.

APPROXIMATE SIZE
48" x 72"

MATERIALS
Lamb's Pride Bulky from Brown Sheep Company (85% wool, 15% mohair; 125 yds;113 g) in the following amounts and colors:

Brown	6 skeins	color M-02 Brown Heather
Blue	3 skeins	color M-82 Blue Flannel
Green	3 skeins	color M-68 Pine Tree
Red	3 skeins	color M-181 Prairie Fire

Size 10½ circular needle (32") or size required to obtain gauge

2 ring markers

GAUGE
12 sts = 4" in patt

DIRECTIONS
Sl 2 wyif: Move yarn to front of work and sl 2 sts purlwise.

Sl 2 wyib: Move yarn to back of work and sl 2 sts purlwise.

- With Brown, CO 146 sts and knit 13 rows.
- Work body of throw as follows:

  Row 1 (RS): With Blue, K8, pm, K130, pm, K8.

  Row 2: With Blue, K8, P130, K8.

  Row 3: With Brown, K8, (sl 2 wyif, K2) across to last 10 sts, sl 2 wyif, K8.

  Row 4: With Brown, K8, P2, (sl 2 wyib, P2) across to last 8 sts, K8.

  Rows 5–12: Rep rows 1–4.

  Row 13: With Blue, knit.

  Row 14: With Blue, K8, P130, K8.

  Rows 15–36: Rep rows 13 and 14.

  Rows 37–46: Rep rows 3–12.

  Rows 47–58: With Brown, rep rows 13 and 14.

  Rows 59–116: Rep rows 1–58, substituting Green for Blue.

  Rows 117–174: Rep rows 1–58, substituting Red for Blue.

  Rows 175–232: Rep rows 1–58 with Blue.

  Rows 233–290: Rep rows 59–116.

  Rows 291–336: Rep rows 1–46, substituting Red for Blue.

- With Brown, knit 13 rows.
- BO sts knitwise.
- Block.

Stained Glass

Easy garter-stitch squares and rectangles are joined with simple crochet in this colorful throw.

APPROXIMATE SIZE
40" x 52"

MATERIALS
Canadiana from Patons (100% acrylic; 228 yds; 100 g) in the following amounts and colors:

4 MEDIUM

Yellow	1 skein	color 95
Purple	1 skein	color 26
Pink	1 skein	color 11
Light Jade	1 skein	color 46
Medium Blue	1 skein	color 30
Royal Blue	4 skeins	color 33

Size 8 needles or size required to obtain gauge

Size G crochet hook

Tapestry needle

GAUGE
16 sts = 4" in garter st

GARTER STITCH
Knit every row.

DIRECTIONS
Small rectangle (4" x 6"): CO 24 sts, work 30 rows in garter st. BO loosely.

Square (6" x 6"): CO 24 sts, work 46 rows in garter st. BO loosely.

Large rectangle (6" x 8"): CO 24 sts, work 62 rows in garter st. BO loosely.

- From **each** of the Yellow, Purple, Pink, Light Jade, and Medium Blue yarns, make 2 small rectangles, 2 squares, and 2 large rectangles, for a total of 30 pieces.

- With crochet hook and Royal Blue, work 1 rnd of sc all around each piece, working 3 sc in each corner, join with sl st into first sc. Work 1 more rnd of sc all around, working into back loops only, join and fasten off.

- Arrange pieces into 5 rows, mixing colors as desired, so that there are 2 small rectangles, 2 squares, and 2 large rectangles in each row. With tapestry needle and Royal Blue, sew squares tog in rows using an overcast st (see card 21). Join rows in same manner.

- **Edging:** With crochet hook, RS facing you, and Royal Blue, work 1 rnd of sc, work 3 rnds of dc in back loop only, then work 1 rnd of sc in back loop only (see card 22).

- Block.

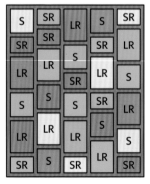

SR = small rectangle

S = square

LR = large rectangle